THE ALPS

CHARLES W. MAYNARD

The Rosen Publishing Group's
PowerKids Press™
New York

*To David, who has scaled the heights of the Alps, the Rockies, the Appalachians,
the Cascades, the Sierra Nevadas, and Kilimanjaro, always in friendship*

Published in 2004 by The Rosen Publishing Group, Inc.
29 East 21st Street, New York, NY 10010

First Edition

Editor: Frances E. Ruffin
Book Design: Emily Muschinske
Photo Researcher: Barbara Koppelman

Photo Credits: Cover and title page © Getty Images, Inc.; p. 4 © Byan F. Peterson/CORBIS; p. 6 © Geo Atlas 2002; p. 7 Earth Scenes © Michael Andrews; p. 7 (inset) © Jonathan Blair/CORBIS; p. 8 (top) © Nature Picture Library; p. 8 (bottom) © 2001 Blaine Harrington III; p. 11 © National Geographic; p. 11 (inset) © Owen Franken/CORBIS; pp. 12, 16 © Simone Huber/Getty Images; p. 15 (top) © Oriol Alamany & E. Vicens/CORBIS; p. 15 (bottom) Animals Animals © D. Valla; p. 19 © Hulton/Archive/Getty Images; p. 19 (Inset) © Araldo de Luca/CORBIS; p. 20 (bottom) © Kenneth Garrett/National Geographic; p. 20 (top) Reuters NewMedia Inc./CORBIS.

Maynard, Charles W. (Charles William), 1955–
The Alps / Charles W. Maynard.
    p. cm.— (Great mountain ranges of the world)
Includes bibliographical references and index.
  ISBN 0-8239-6697-6
1. Alps—Juvenile literature. I. Title.
  DQ823 .M34 2004
  914.94'7—dc21

                                          2002013500

Manufactured in the United States of America

CONTENTS

4

Mountains and Meadows

The Alps tower over many regions of Western Europe. Many people live in the deep valleys of the Alps. The mountain chain gets its name from its grassy meadows, not from its snowy peaks. For centuries, alps were what these people called the high, grassy meadows in these mountains.

The Alps make a 660-mile (1,062-km) arc through south central Europe. The mountains are about 125 miles (201 km) wide. These high, snow-covered peaks are made of many smaller ranges that stretch from Hungary in eastern Europe to France and Italy in western Europe. The Alps are split into three ranges. The western range runs from the Savoy Alps in France to the Maritime Alps between France and Italy. The central Alps go from the Bernese Alps in Switzerland's northern range to the Pennine Alps in the south. The eastern range runs from the Dinaric Alps to the Noric Alps in Austria. Mont Blanc is on the border between France and Italy. At 15,771 feet (4,807 m) above **sea level**, it is Europe's highest peak.

The little girl in this photo is in a meadow near the village of Cordon, France. The French Alps are shown rising in the distance.

YOUNG MOUNTAINS

The Alps are folded mountains, which means that many layers of rock created them. Some of the rock that makes up the Alps was formed more than 130 million years ago at the bottom of a sea. The African and European **plates** on Earth's **crust** moved slowly toward each other, pushing up the land and pushing out the sea into high mountains. One mountain-building bump took place only 5 million years ago. This means that the Alps are young mountains when compared to other mountain chains, such as the Appalachians in the United States. Clues that the rock formed on the sea floor have been found high in the mountains. Round, flat **fossils** of seashells from creatures called ammonites, 2 feet (.6 m) wide, have been discovered in the Alps.

MOUNTAIN

FACT

MAJOR RANGES OF THE ALPS FROM WEST TO EAST ARE THE HOHE TAUERN ALPS, DOLOMITES, JULIAN ALPS, BERNESE ALPS, LEPONTINE ALPS, RHAETIAN ALPS, DAUPHINÉ ALPS, AND SAVOY ALPS.

These fossils once held large creatures known as ammonites. They were found in rock that makes up the Alps. Millions of years ago, that rock was at the bottom of a sea.

The jagged peaks of the Alps show that, during the mountain-building process, they became folded mountains.

Switzerland's Grosse Aletsch is the longest glacier in the Alps at 17 miles (27 km).

Grapes that will be made into wine grow near Lake Geneva in Switzerland.

Rivers of Ice

Millions of years ago, the Alps were almost 4 miles (6 km) high. Over time, **erosion** began to wear down the mountains. Ice, wind, and water all worked to shape the mountains into the peaks that exist today.

The Alps have many **glaciers**, which can become like rivers of ice. Glaciers begin high on the sides of the snowy peaks. Many years of heavy snowfall create layers of packed snow. The packed snow turns into ice. Eventually, this ice slowly moves down the mountains into the valleys below. As a glacier moves along, it carries rock, gravel, and sand that grind away the mountain. Thousands of years ago, glaciers carved out steep-sided valleys or left behind small hills or ridges of rock called **moraines**. Sometimes hollow moraines fill with water and form lakes. The Alps have many beautiful lakes, including Lake Geneva in Switzerland, that were created by glaciers. Several great rivers began as melting snow in the mountains. The Rhone, Rhine, Inn, and Drava Rivers all have had their start in the melting snows high in the Alps.

CLIMATE ZONES

The **climate** of the Alps changes greatly from sea level on the southeastern coast of France to the towering peak of Mont Blanc. Warm breezes from the Mediterranean and Adriatic Seas blow across the lower parts of the Alps in their southern slopes. They create a **subtropical** climate. The north side of the Alps receives about 120 inches (305 cm) of **precipitation** each year. As this snow melts, it provides water for the valleys and plains beyond the Alps. Many regions of Europe depend on the Alps to supply enough water for their cities and farms.

The highest peaks in the Alps are covered with snow year-round. This polar zone has few plants and animals. There is less **oxygen** at the top of Mont Blanc and other high peaks than at sea level. This lack of oxygen and the very cold weather make it difficult for plants to grow and for humans to live there.

MOUNTAIN FACT

SNOWFALL CAN BE MEASURED BY HOW MUCH WATER IT WOULD MAKE IF IT WERE TO MELT. USUALLY FROM 10 TO 12 INCHES (25–30 CM) OF SNOW IS THE SAME AS 1 INCH (2.5 CM) OF WATER. IN THE NORTHERN ALPS, A 100-INCH (254-CM) SNOWFALL COULD MEAN UP TO 1,200 INCHES (3,048 CM) OF WATER!

Hikers follow a path across a snowy field in the French Alps. Inset: White wildflowers cover the Valley of Marvels between France and Italy.

Alpine Trees and Flowers

A variety of trees and plants grows in the different climate zones of the Alps. The warm hills and the deep valleys around these mountains are covered with olive, oak, beech, spruce, and hornbeam trees. Higher in the mountain are mountain maple, and larch, pine, and other fir trees.

The high grassy meadows, or alps, where sheep and cattle feed, have many wildflowers throughout the summer. The high-**elevation** wildflowers have waxy leaves that protect them from the cold nights. Many shrubs and wildflowers make this part of the Alps very colorful during the short summer.

The tree line, beyond which no trees will grow, is about 7,000 feet (2,134 m) above sea level. In this alpine **tundra** region, the growing season lasts for only three to four months. The snow line, where there is always snow, begins from 8,000 to 10,000 feet (2,438–3,048 m). Very little grows above this line. The weather is severe, and what little soil exists is of poor quality.

 The lacy, white edelweiss is a wildflower that has become known as the flower of the Alps.

High-Elevation Animals

For many hundreds of years, animals such as sheep, goats, and cattle have fed on the grasses of the Alps in the summer. During cold weather, they move to the warmer valleys.

Wild animals that are at home in the high Alps include the snow grouse, the snow mouse, the woodchuck, the ibex, and the chamois, a goatlike antelope. The ibex is a wild goat that lives in the rocky cliffs between the tree line and the snow line, eating the few kinds of plants that grow there. Its huge, curved horns are from 28 to 55 inches (71–140 cm) long. It has an ability to leap from one rocky ledge to another. Males can grow to be 3.4 feet (1 m) tall. The alpine jackdaw, a large black bird related to the crow, lives in the high mountains year-round. Other birds live in the mountains during the summer but make their home in the valleys during the very cold winters.

MOUNTAIN FACT

THE CHAMOIS IS AN ANTELOPE THAT MANY PEOPLE HUNT FOR SKINS. THE CHAMOIS IS AN ENDANGERED SPECIES, OR A KIND OF ANIMAL THAT IS IN DANGER OF DYING OUT IF WE DON'T PROTECT IT. THE CHAMOIS IS NOW PROTECTED IN SWISS NATIONAL PARK.

Top: *Alpine ibexes cross mountain rocks in Valais, Switzerland. Bottom: An alpine marmot suns himself on a cliff in the French Alps.*

THE WORLD'S PLAYGROUND

From east to west, the Alps lie in Yugoslavia, Austria, Germany, Liechtenstein, Switzerland, France, and Italy. More than 20 million people live in the valleys of this mountainous region. Many languages are spoken throughout the area. In Switzerland alone, the people may speak several languages, including German, Italian, French, and Romansh, a language that is similar to Latin.

The major business of the area is **tourism**. The beautiful scenery attracts more than 100 million people from all over the world each year. These tourists come to ski, hike, snowboard, and climb mountains. Others tour pretty little villages. Tourism makes this region of Europe a wealthy area where people have well-paying jobs. In France, sheep are herded along a 175-mile (282-km) route to the rich, grassy alpine meadows in an annual event called the transhumance. The herders and their sheep make this two-week journey that **generations** before them have made.

The people on this ski lift, in the Dolomites of the Italian Alps, are among the millions of people who travel to the Alps for some of the world's best ski slopes.

Conquering the Alps

Thousands of years ago, hunters followed **game** through mountain passes into the high meadows and made their homes there. People have lived in the Alps ever since.

In 218 B.C., Hannibal, a North African general from Carthage, led an army of 40,000 soldiers through the Alps to attack Rome. His army included elephants and mules. Many men and animals died on the 15-day march through the snow and ice. However, he did reach Italy. Famous military leaders and their armies have made the difficult crossing since then. Some of the roads through the passes that were paved by Roman soldiers in the first century B.C. are still in use today.

In recent times, mountain climbers have **conquered** all the peaks in the Alps. Michel-Gabriel Paccard and Jacques Balmat were the first to climb Mont Blanc in 1786. In 1865, Edward Whymper scaled the "unconquerable" Matterhorn peak.

MOUNTAIN FACT

Mont Blanc was first scaled in 1786. Climbers first reached the top of Monta Rosa in 1855. The towering Matterhorn, once considered to be an "unconquerable" peak, was climbed in 1865.

Below: The painting by Italian painter, Raphael, shows Hannibal on an elephant fighting Roman soldiers as he crossed the Alps.

Right: English mountaineer Edward Whymper was photographed with the climbing gear that he carried and wore when he scaled the Matterhorn in 1865.

19

Above: *The Ice Man is the mummy of a man that was found frozen in the ice between Italy and Austria in 1999. Believed to have lived 5,000 years ago, he may become a new Alp legend.*
Right: *Scientists have reconstructed the face of the Ice Man to show how he might have looked.*

THE STORIED ALPS

The Alps are mountains of history and **legend**. One favorite story for children around the world is *Heidi* by Johanna Spyri. This novel, first published in 1880–1881, tells the tale of Heidi, who grew up in the high meadows raising sheep and goats with her grandfather. Spyri wrote from her own experiences as a girl growing up in the mountains near Zurich, Switzerland.

William Tell's story is only a legend told among alpine villagers, but for many people it seems based on fact. According to the legend, during the 1300s, Tell refused to remove his cap and show respect to a government official. He was then ordered to shoot an apple from his son's head. Fortunately, Tell's shot struck the apple, and his son was unharmed.

During the early days of **World War II**, the von Trapp family of Austria traveled over the Alps to Switzerland to escape from the **Nazis**. Their story has been made into a musical play and movie, *The Sound of Music*.

Deep in the Alps

In the 1800s, the scientific study of mountains around the world began in the Alps. **Geologists** began to look closely at the rocks and the structures of the mountains to understand better how they were made.

The Romans first built roads through the passes of the Alps in the first century B.C. Since then other people have constructed roads and railroads through steep valleys and over high passes. A number of tunnels were carved out of the mountains to allow traffic to flow year-round. One of the world's longest tunnels goes through Mont Blanc. The 7.2-mile (12-km) tunnel was built by workers from France and Italy. Each team started in its own country. When workers from the two countries met in the middle on August 14, 1962, their halves of the tunnel were only 9 inches (23 cm) off center. The tunnel was completed in 1964.

In September 1991, two hikers walking in the Alps at 10,530 feet (3,210 m) found the frozen body of a man who had lived 5,000 years ago. This **mummy** was called the Ice Man. Scientists have carefully studied the Ice Man to learn more about people during the time in which he lived.

GLOSSARY

climate (KLY-mit) The kind of weather a certain area has.

conquered (KON-kerd) To have overcome something.

crust (KRUST) The outer, or top, layer of a planet. Earth's crust is broken up into many pieces.

elevation (eh-luh-VAY-shun) The height of an object.

erosion (ih-ROH-zhun) To be worn away slowly.

fossils (FAH-sulz) The hardened remains of a dead animal or plant.

game (GAYM) Wild animals that are hunted for food.

generations (jeh-nuh-RAY-shunz) All the people who are born in the same period.

geologists (jee-AH-luh-jists) Scientists who study the structure of Earth.

glaciers (GLAY-shurz) Large masses of ice that move down a mountain or along a valley.

legend (LEH-jend) A story, passed down through the years, that cannot be proven.

moraines (muh-RAYNZ) Hills of earth and stones left behind by a glacier.

mummy (MUH-mee) A dead body that has been kept from rotting.

Nazis (NOT-seez) Members of the German army under the leadership of Adolf Hitler.

oxygen (OK-sih-jen) A gas that has no color, taste, or odor and is necessary for people and animals to breathe.

plates (PLAYTS) The moving pieces of Earth's crust.

precipitation (preh-sih-pih-TAY-shun) Any moisture that falls from the sky.

sea level (SEE LEH-vul) The height of the top of the ocean.

subtropical (sub-TRAH-pih-kul) Just outside the warmest parts of Earth.

tourism (TUR-ih-zem) A business that deals with people who travel for pleasure.

tundra (TUN-druh) The frozen land of the coldest parts of the world.

World War II (WURLD WOR TOO) A war fought by the United States, Great Britain, and Russia against Germany, Japan, and Italy from 1939 to 1945.

INDEX

WEB SITES

Due to the changing nature of Internet links, PowerKids Press has developed an online list of Web sites related to the subject of this book. This site is updated regularly. Please use this link to access the list:

www.powerkidslinks.com/gmrw/alps/